The adventure begins...

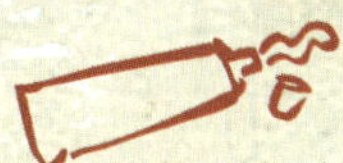

Preparing to go

Things to remember...

to take (tick them off as you go)

( ) Passport

( ) Money

( ) Plug adapter

( ) Toiletries

( ) Sun cream

( ) Sunglasses

( ) Comfortable walking shoes

( ) Travel guidebook

( ) Phrasebook

( ) Warm clothing (for cold nights)

to do (tick them off as you go)

(✓) Check my passport is valid and in date

(✓) Read up on my destination and find out about its local laws and customs

(✓) Check with my doctor whether I need any vaccinations

(✓) Arrange for someone to look after my pet(s)

( ) Get travel insurance

( ) Order currency for my trip

( ) Take some back-up funds, such as travellers cheques

( ) Make copies of my passport, ticket details and insurance policy's 24-hour emergency number to leave with my family or friends

(✓) Leave a copy of my itinerary and contact details with family and friends

"Own only what you can carry with you;
let your memory be your travel bag."

ALEXANDER SOLZHENITSYN

Tomorrow I begin my travels and I'm feeling:

My goals for this trip are:

learn about thai culture and
See how the locals live,
feed elephants and monkeys !!!

The people I'll be thinking about on my trip:

(Stick a photo of your loved one here)

(Stick a photo of your loved one here)

(Stick a photo of your loved one here)

Travel plans

The journey begins...

(Stick a photo here of yourself ready to set off)

The intrepid traveller!

"A journey of a thousand miles
begins with a single step."

CONFUCIUS

What a day:

"One's destination is never a place
but rather a new way of looking at things."

HENRY MILLER

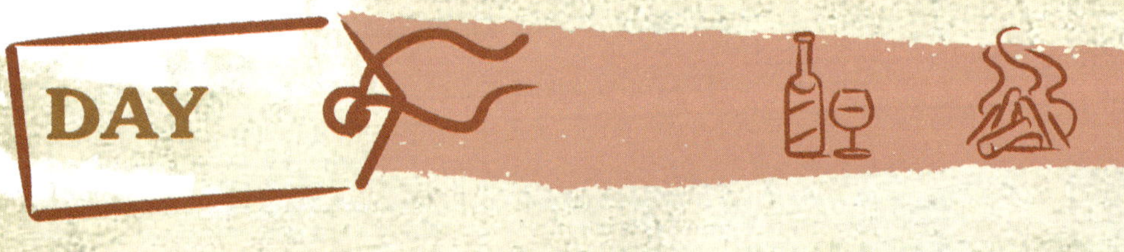

A day to remember:

About this shot:

"The World is a book, and those who do not travel read only a page."

ST. AUGUSTINE

Time to reflect:

Today's news...

...And views

DAY
410

Dear diary...

"I travel not to go anywhere, but to go.
I travel for travel's sake. The great affair is to move."

ROBERT LOUIS STEVENSON

The adventure continues...

Picture perfect:

Eateries

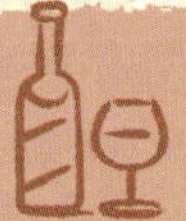

Memorable food-stops of the trip...

Eatery

Location

Type of food

The meal

Star rating

Eatery

Location

Type of food

The meal

Star rating

Talking points

(Photo or business card here)

Star rating

0* Never go back 1* OK in desperation 2* Filled a gap 3* Nothing to write home about 4* Would go back 5* Worth shouting about

Eatery

Location

Type of food

The meal

Star rating

Eatery

Location

Type of food

The meal

Star rating

Talking points

"Part of the secret of success in life is to eat what you like and let the food fight it out inside."

MARK TWAIN

Eateries

Star rating
0* Never go back 1* OK in desperation 2* Filled a gap 3* Nothing to write home about 4* Would go back 5* Worth shouting about

Eatery

Location

Type of food

The meal

Star rating

Eatery

Location

Type of food

The meal

Star rating

Talking points

"No man is lonely eating spaghetti;
it requires so much attention."

CHRISTOPHER MORLEY

"All happiness depends on a leisurely breakfast."

JOHN GUNTHER

Eatery

Location

Type of food

The meal

Star rating

Eatery

Location

Type of food

The meal

Star rating

Talking points

DAY

"A good traveller has no fixed plans,
and is not intent on arriving."

LAO TZU

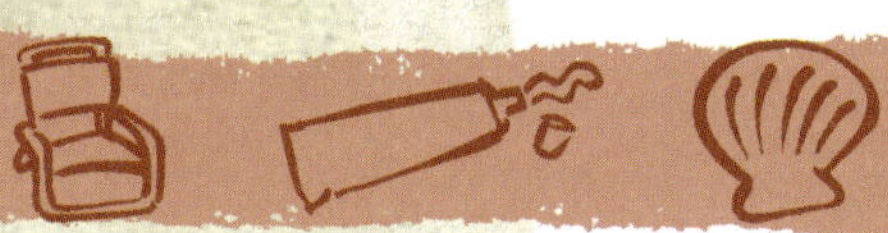

Thoughts of the day:

Today's news...

...And views

DAY

Health Tips

Food & drink...

Drink bottled water or sterilise water by boiling or using purification tablets.

Avoid ice in drinks unless you're sure it's made from treated, chlorinated water.

Avoid ice cream and lollies from kiosks or street traders.

Avoid unpasteurised milk.

Avoid uncooked food unless you can peel or shell it yourself.

Make sure food has been freshly and thoroughly cooked and is still piping hot.

Sun & heat...

Stay out of direct sunlight in the hottest part of the day (usually between 11am and 3pm).

Don't get sunburned – red skin means it's been damaged.

Use factor 15+ sunscreen.

Cover up children.

Babies should never be exposed to direct sunlight.

Don't do anything too energetic in the hottest part of the day and drink plenty of water.

Swimming...

Never go swimming alone.

Never leave children unattended in, or near, water.

Try not to swallow water while you swim.

Check the depth of water before you dive.

Insect & animal bites...

Use an insect repellent and keep your arms and legs covered in areas with mosquitoes and other biting insects.

Seek medical treatment if a bite becomes swollen or infected.

Never feed or stroke wild animals (this includes cats and dogs) as they may have rabies.

If an animal bites you, seek medical attention immediately.

Organise travel insurance before you go on holiday, and for visits to European countries, don't forget your European Health Insurance Card (EHIC).

"Health is not valued till sickness comes."

DR. THOMAS FULLER

DAY
Click, click:

The day's events:

> "Travel and change of place
> impart new vigour to the mind."
>
> **SENECA**

A traveller's tales:

Snap Happy:

Watering Holes

My favourite bars...

Name of bar

Location

Why it's 'the Biz'

Name of bar

Location

Why it's 'the Biz'

Name of bar

Location

Why it's 'the Biz'

(Photo or business card here)

Name of bar

Location

Why it's 'the Biz'

Name of bar

Location

Why it's 'the Biz'

Name of bar

Location

Why it's 'the Biz'

"One martini is all right.
Two are too many, and three are not enough."

JAMES THURBER

Watering Holes

Name of bar

Location

Why it's 'the Biz'

Name of bar

Location

Why it's 'the Biz'

Name of bar

Location

Why it's 'the Biz'

"Good company and good discourse are the very sinews of virtue."

IZAAK WALTON

Name of bar

Location

Why it's 'the Biz'

Name of bar

Location

Why it's 'the Biz'

Name of bar

Location

Why it's 'the Biz'

DAY

What I've been up to...

"Half the fun of the travel is the aesthetic of lostness."

RAY BRADBURY

Today's news...

...And views

DAY
More about the photos...

Thoughts of the day:

"If you reject the food, ignore the customs, fear the religion and avoid the people, you might better stay home."

JAMES MICHENER

How I spent my time:

Captured on film:

"I dislike feeling at home when I am abroad."

GEORGE BERNARD SHAW

Dear diary...

A day to remember:

Photo call:

Tickets

Travel tickets...

(Stick plane, bus, tram
& train tickets here)

(Stick plane, bus, tram
& train tickets here)

"We wander for distraction,
but we travel for fulfilment."

HILAIRE BELLOC

Tickets

Entrance tickets...

(Stick entrance tickets to museums, galleries & attractions here)

"Like all great travellers, I have seen more than I remember, and remember more than I have seen."

BENJAMIN DISRAELI

(Stick entrance tickets to museums,
galleries & attractions here)

My gallery:

What a day:

"The most important trip you may take in
life is meeting people halfway."

HENRY BOYE

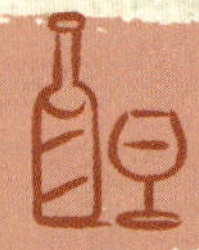

Moments to savour:

Camera action:

DAY

"The traveller sees what he sees.
The tourist sees what he has come to see."

G.K. CHESTERTON

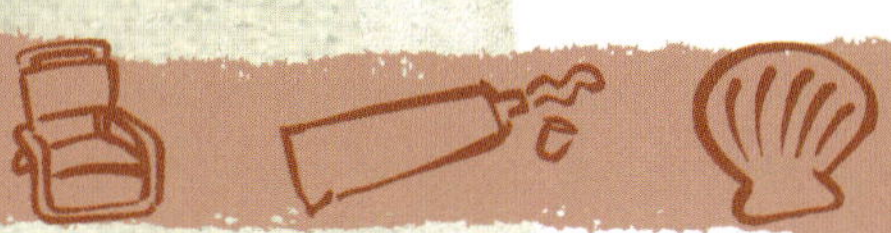

Today's exploits:

Today's news...

...And views

Activities

Exciting things I've done so far...

Day

Location

Activity

Memories

Day

Location

Activity

Memories

"Adventure is a state of mind — and spirit."

JACQUELINE COCHRAN

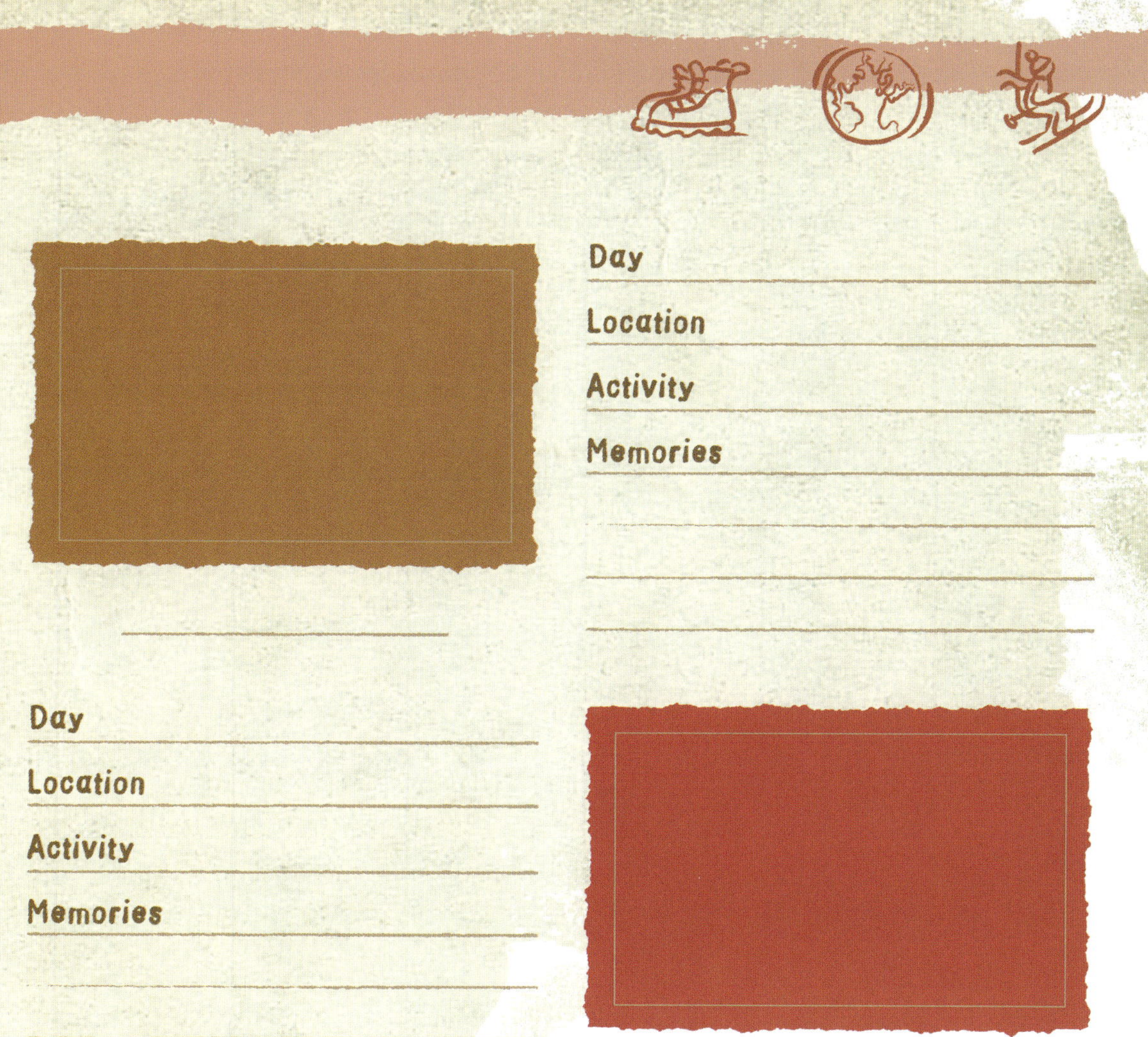

"One way to get the most out of life
is to look upon it as an adventure."

WILLIAM FEATHER

Out & About...

Through the lens:

DAY
Caught on camera:

Time to reflect:

"Tourists don't know where they've been,
travellers don't know where they're going."

PAUL THEROUX

News...

And what a view:

"All journeys have secret destinations of which the traveller is unaware."

MARTIN BUBER

Journal entry:

How I spent my time:

Snap Happy:

Buildings

My favourite landmarks of the trip...

Day

Location

Landmark

Interesting facts

Day

Location

Landmark

Interesting facts

Day

Location

Landmark

Interesting facts

Day

Location

Landmark

Interesting facts

"The physician can bury his mistakes, but the architect can only advise his client to plant vines..."

FRANK LLOYD WRIGHT

Natural Beauty

Breathtaking scenes...

Day Location

Scene

"Beauty is truth, truth beauty,' — that is all
Ye know on earth, and all ye need to know."

JOHN KEATS

Day

Location

Scene

Day

Location

Scene

DAY
About these photos:

Pen to *paper*:

"It may be that the satisfaction I need
depends on my going away, so that when
I've gone and come back, I'll find it at home."

RUMI

DAY
My musings:

What a day:

"If you want to succeed you should strike out on new paths, rather than travel the worn paths of accepted success."

JOHN D. ROCKEFELLER

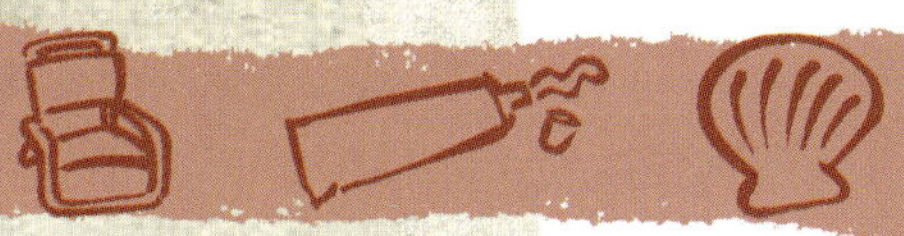

Moments to savour:

Today's news...

...And views

Journeys

My most interesting travel experiences of the trip...

To

From

By

On day

Talking points

To

From

By

On day

Talking points

To

From

By

On day

Talking points

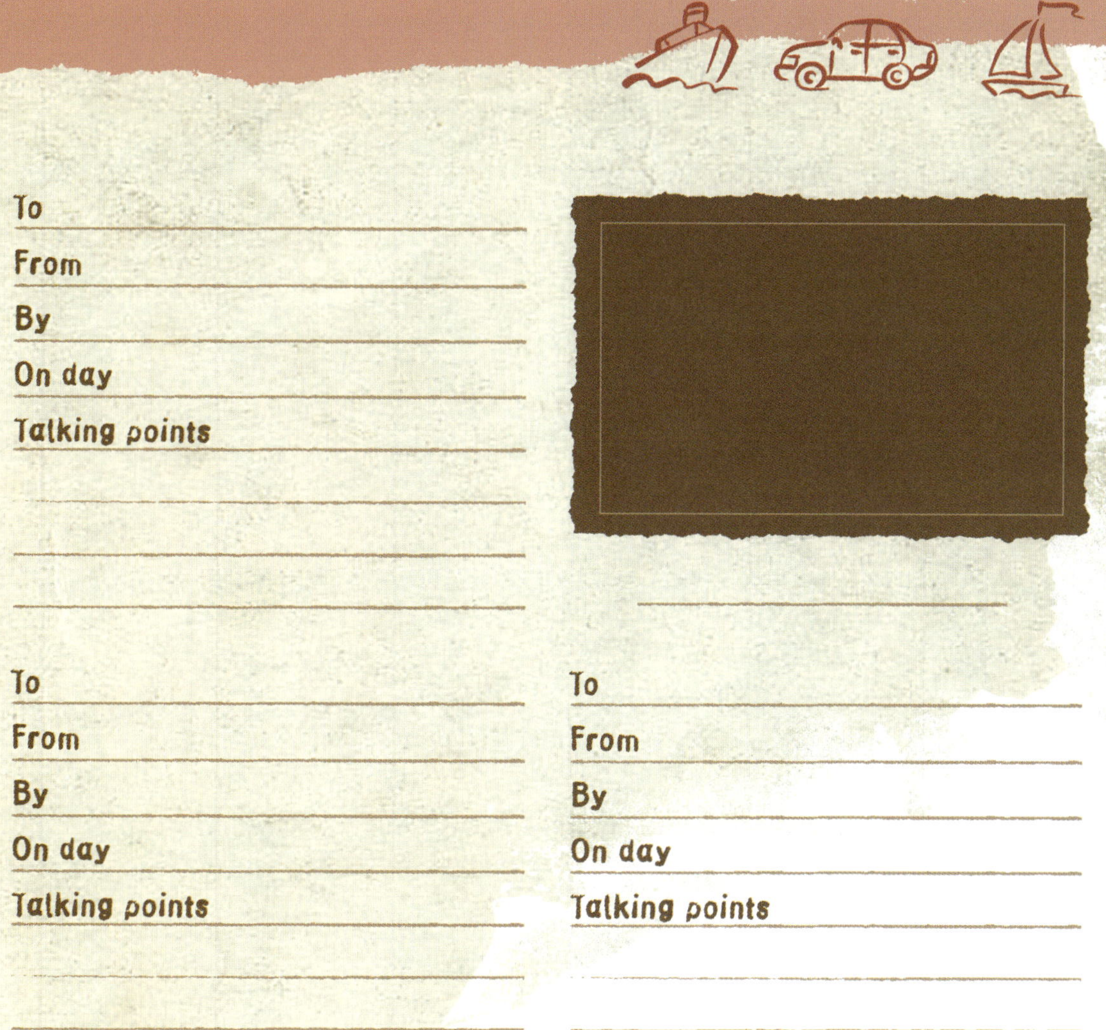

"The only way of catching a train I ever discovered is to miss the train before."

G.K. CHESTERTON

The adventure continues...

Picture perfect:

DAY
Hall of fame:

A day to remember:

> "Travel can be one of the most
> rewarding forms of introspection."
>
> LAURENCE DURRELL

The adventure continues...

A picture says a thousand words:

"No one realizes how beautiful it is to travel until he comes home and rests his head on his old, familiar pillow."

LIN YUTANG

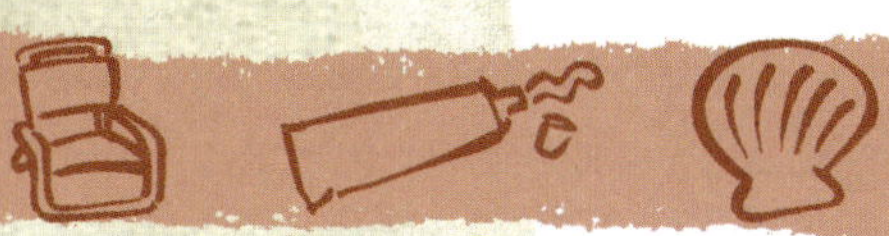

So near the end:

Time to reflect:

More about these piccies:

DAY

Dear diary...

"He who would travel happily must travel light."

ANTOINE DE ST. EXUPERY

Final thoughts...

About this shot:

Photos

"Good company in a journey
makes the way seem shorter."

IZAAK WALTON

Photos

Photos

"A journey is best measured in friends, rather than miles."

TIM CAHILL

Photos

WAY

Notes

Notes

Notes

WAY

Notes

Notes

Measurements & Conversions

Metric to Imperial

DISTANCE

1 millimetre (mm)		= 0.0394 inches (in)
1 centimetre (cm)	= 10 mm	= 0.3937 in
1 metre (m)	= 100 cm	= 1.0936 yds
1 kilometre (km)	= 1000 cm	= 0.6214 mile

AREA

1 sq cm (cm^2)	= 100 mm^2	= 0.1550 in^2
1 sq metre (m^2)	= 10,000 cm^2	= 1.1960 yd^2
1 hectare (ha)	= 10,000 m^2	= 2.4711 acres
1 sq km (km^2)	= 100 ha	= 0.3861 $mile^2$

WEIGHT

1 milligram (mg)		= 0.0154 grain (gr)
1 gram (g)	= 1000 mg	= 0.0353 oz
1 (kg)	= 1000 g	= 2.2046 lb
1 tonne (t)	= 1000 kg	= 0.9842 ton

Imperial to Metric

DISTANCE

1 inch (in)		= 2.54 cm
1 foot (ft)	= 12 in	= 0.3048 m
1 yard (yd)	= 3 ft	= 0.9144 m
1 mile	= 1760 yd	= 1.6093 km
1 int naut. mile	= 2025.4 yd	= 1.852 km

AREA

1 sq inch (in^2)		= 6.4516 cm^2
1 sq yard (yd^2)	= 9 ft^2	= 0.8361 m^2
1 acre	= 4840 yd^2	= 4046.9 m^2
1 sq mile ($mile^2$)	= 640 acres	= 2.59 km^2

WEIGHT

1 ounce (oz)	= 437.5 gr	= 28.35 g
1 pound (lb)	= 16 oz	= 0.4536 kg
1 hundredweight (cwt)	= 112 lb	= 50.802 kg
1 ton	= 20 cwt	= 1.016 t

TEMPERATURE
Celsius/Fahrenheit

Names & Addresses

Name:

Address:

Tel:

Email:

Notes:

Name:

Address:

Tel:

Email:

Notes:

Name:

Address:

Tel:

Email:

Notes:

Name:

Address:

Tel:

Email:

Notes:

Name:

Address:

Tel:

Email:

Notes:

Name:

Address:

Tel:

Email:

Notes:

Names & Addresses

Name:

Address:

Tel:

Email:

Notes:

Name:

Address:

Tel:

Email:

Notes:

Name:

Address:

Tel:

Email:

Notes:

Name:

Address:

Tel:

Email:

Notes:

Name:

Address:

Tel:

Email:

Notes:

Name:

Address:

Tel:

Email:

Notes:

Name:

Address:

Tel:

Email:

Notes:

Name:

Address:

Tel:

Email:

Notes:

Name:

Address:

Tel:

Email:

Notes:

Name:

Address:

Tel:

Email:

Notes:

"A good traveller is one who does not know where he is going to, and a perfect traveller does not know where he came from."

LIN YUTANG

Names & Addresses

Name:

Address:

Tel:

Email:

Notes:

Name:

Address:

Tel:

Email:

Notes:

Name:

Address:

Tel:

Email:

Notes:

Name:

Address:

Tel:

Email:

Notes:

Name:

Address:

Tel:

Email:

Notes:

Name:

Address:

Tel:

Email:

Notes:

Name:

Address:

Tel:

Email:

Notes:

Name:

Address:

Tel:

Email:

Notes:

Name:

Address:

Tel:

Email:

Notes:

Name:

Address:

Tel:

Email:

Notes:

Name:

Address:

Tel:

Email:

Notes:

Name:

Address:

Tel:

Email:

Notes:

...The end of my journey